The Winding Path of a Shero's Journey

Xulon Press Elite
2301 Lucien Way #415
Maitland, FL 32751
407.339.4217
www.xulonpress.com

Paperback ISBN-13: 978-1-6628-7467-3
Dust Jacket ISBN-13: 978-1-6628-7468-0
Ebook ISBN-13: 978-1-6628-7776-6

"The author, Carolyn Coles Benton, perfectly captures the vicissitudes of the life of a woman of God, and parallels the rise of the denomination, Church of God in Christ. This biography also includes timely and valuable discussions of women's health issues."

"With chills and tears, I read the story of a woman who triumphed over adversities and still did not bend or break, but stood strong through her faith in God. This is a great overview of the origin and role of the Black Church, especially the Church of God in Christ."

"…a compelling story of inspiration and resilience; a guide for all. Profound leadership skills developed during Ella's formative years. She built onto her father's legacy from day one! This story gets to the heart of faith, family, respect, and concrete judgment skills. Her kinship roots carried her through her journey of life. This narrative should be read by others because it encourages and enlightens women of all levels. Life has many challenges and choices that we all face; however, some— much like Ella—prevail on the high road."

"Aunt Ella's story inspires. It motivates. It encourages. It makes you cry and laugh. It causes you to be thankful. It makes you angry. But, reading this book, you will walk away quoting the words of Marvin Sapp, "I 'm stronger, I'm wiser, I'm better…"Aunt Ella's story is one of turning adversities into opportunities. She also reminds us that when you trust in God, all things are possible.

Now, I understand our connection. Aunt Ella is a woman who does not make excuses, much like me. She keeps moving in the face of adversity. Obstacles become challenges.

She lets nothing disturb her faith. If you read her book, you will put it down believing that you can move mountains and knowing that you can make it.

Thank you, Aunt Ella, for sharing your journey."

—Judge Mablean Ephriam (Friend of Ella Gordon),
Long Beach, CA

"The path woven by Ella B. (Agnew) Gordon was filled with brilliance, creativity, and abiding faith. The legacy handed down from her family—who were ancestors of enslavement—includes freedom and spirituality, and a progression in Ella's church work. She was equipped for thundering success, paving the way for women with her courage, love, spirituality, and her will to remain her authentic self. As her peer, it (the story) filled me with pride in anticipation of her future. It is evident that she is not finished with her work yet."

–Allie Howell Freeman, ACSW-R, Buffalo, NY

"This book will help you understand how important it is to pay close attention to every experience on your journey through life. After all is said, Ella Gordon expresses three lessons: 1) Management skills in business, 2) Excellence in all one's endeavors, and 3) Outstanding fashion par excellence for a first class Christian woman."

–Bishop Clarence B. and Dr. Joyce R. Haddon
(Friends of Ella Gordon), Detroit, MI

"This story impacted me as a hands-on observer. While visiting Marrakech for the incredible Talbi Wedding in 2019, you and Ella connected and bonded like it was ordained. To note your inspiration to pursue writing this book about her (Ella) was singularly miraculous! Thus, my gratification on being there at the genesis of and collaboration on this work of art. I connect with the chapters throughout Ella's life and it is illuminating. I absolutely recommend reading this wonderful book to many others."

–Desma Reid-Coleman, Owner of St. J. Style Inc.
Designer ReSale, Detroit, Michigan

"A fearless woman of wisdom, poise, and elegance with God's favor! Ella is unrelenting in her pursuit to conquer every challenge she faces. I continue to be amazed by her tenacious spirit, inspired by her courage, and uplifted by her compassion. This book is a master class in survival and determination."

–Elder Steven Sledge (Brother-Friend of Ella Gordon), Dallas, TX

"*The Winding Path of a Shero's Journey* is a story of a renaissance woman and a dear friend shaped from perseverance and strength against life's tribulations and iniquities. Ella's life story is an inspiring testament to her faith that has never wavered. I have known Ella for over three decades, sharing our ups and downs. She has had tremendous losses; however, she remains tenacious and strong in spirit through her faith."

–Luke Song (Friend of Ella Gordon), Farmington Hills, MI

The *Winding Path*

of a
Shero's
Journey

Carolyn Coles Benton
Foreword by Presiding Bishop J. Drew Sheard, Sr.

XULON ELITE

Dedication

To my children, with unconditional love:
Taheera and Louis

In memory of my grandfather:
Bishop Sylvester C. Coles, Sr.
"The Sunday School Man"
1899–1992

"The spirit of God is moving in the earth.
For every right desire, there is an answer.
Lord, increase my faith." –S. C. C.

Foreword

THIS BOOK WILL move you to a point of celebrating a story of how God can instill in a person of obscurity the will, the determination, and the drive to succeed. This compelling story will take you from crying tears of compassion to laughing with joy, rooting for Ella to keep going where God will take her.

I am extremely blessed to have observed Ella Gordon as my beautiful, classy, and unstoppable aunt; a diligent churchwoman and undeniable "go-getter." Her story—from almost rags to riches in Christ Jesus—needs to be told for every "single mother" and every "struggling saint" to gain strength from.

Her story from the major obstacles of health to this now articulate, motivating, and inspiring woman of God is a testament of the scripture: *…If God be for us, who can be against us?* (Romans 8:31 KJV). Read and enjoy!

Presiding-Bishop J. Drew Sheard, Sr., Senior Pastor
Greater Emmanuel Institutional Church of God in Christ
Detroit, Michigan

Preface

THE TRANSFORMATIONAL STORY of a living shero privileged me with an opportunity to tell of a journey and its continuing challenges that defined the character of a God-fearing woman surviving in the twentieth century. This woman worked with her hands and led with her heart which took her on a perpetual course of adversity from young adulthood to her prime when she determinedly—through career, marriage, childbirth, entrepreneurship, pitfalls, and afflictions—submitted to the will of God to direct her path in all circumstances.

With a sense of purpose and tenacity, she evolved into a visionary leader who continues to thrive, even more so as a savvy Christian senior. To listen to her tell of growing a denominational prayer breakfast into a much anticipated annual spiritual feast that consistently attracts hundreds of attendees is enthralling. She—who is charismatic, full of life, refined, optimistic, and quite independent—has totally allowed her faith to be the footing that balances and supports her day-to-day path through life.

Her name is Ella Belle Agnew Gordon. Her portraiture is one of love. She graciously displays it along with a combination of care, commitment, respect, and trust as she gifted me with her story. I am inspired by her love that has transcended into a meaningful connection through faith and prayer while she ministered to me during my three-month recovery from COVID-19. There is power in prayer and even more power in a praying woman. Ella's faith in God's healing power has been the nemesis of an extended reconnection of my own spiritual formation as a Christian. Our winding transformational walk—connecting as sisters in Christ—has eloquently delivered to me her prevailing testimony: God triumphs in the end. For this reason, with gratitude and grace, I share HERstory.

Carolyn Coles Benton

Table of Contents

Introduction

IT IS RELEVANT for the reader, whether unfamiliar or acquainted with a specific denomination, to realize the significance of one's chosen religious affiliation and acknowledge the impact it may perhaps have on one's lifestyle, family dynamic, circle of influence, or cultural community.

With over six million members globally, the Church of God in Christ (COGIC) is one of the largest Pentecostal denominations established. Having an early start in the 1700s, the Black Baptist Church (later forming the National Baptist Convention, USA, Inc.) has been recorded as the largest Black organization in terms of membership, boasting around 7.5 million members. One of the earliest formations of the Black Pentecostal Movement occurred in 1897 as an offspring from a Black Holiness sect called the Church of God in Christ.1

Bishop Charles Harrison Mason Sr., founder and first senior bishop of the Church of God in Christ, believed in charismatic preaching, the inward dwelling of the Holy Ghost, righteous living, and total dedication to God. Unlike the Black Baptist Church and the African Methodist Episcopal Church, the Church of God in Christ is the only Black Christian denomination in America that was solely birthed from the African American religious experience without being a byproduct of White Christian denomination.

The primary purpose of this comprehensive historical overview of the Church of God in Christ is reflective of personal experiences that illustrate its finite structure. By highlighting its formation, development, and transition from the established Black Christian church body in America onto a highly energetic style of preaching to the world, the Church of God in Christ is an electrifying worship experience, at best. It was funded, organized, and has been fully controlled by African-Americans since 1897, and remains spiritually-charged, much like its founder, Bishop Charles Harrison Mason, Sr. Notably.

The culture of the COCIG begins with delivering the Word of God, which is often performed by a leader who claims a God-appointed mandate to preach to the masses. The delivery is charismatic and spirit-filled. During worship on any given Sunday, the service might be characterized as one of high praise that is drawn out by holy dancing (dancing in the spirit), shouting (both in a supplicatory or celebratory manner), and voluntary evangelizing God's Word based on the truth of Scripture and the church. All of these are considered integral practices of this Holiness-Pentecostal group that had a major impact on the religious forces in the United States as well as around the world.

Founding Bishop Charles Harrison Mason was born September 8, 1866 in Shelby County, Tennessee. His parents, Jerry and Eliza Mason, were ex-slaves and members of the African American Missionary Baptist Church. Mason was greatly influenced by his parents and their friends who would become his followers. He served from 1907 until his death in 1961. As a result of his leadership, the denomination built Mason Temple Church of God in Christ in Memphis, Tennessee, which—again—was financed by Black church members that included sharecroppers, cotton pickers, and even domestic servants.

As far back as 1906, Bishop Charles Harrison Mason, Sr. recognized the equality and tremendous value of women working throughout the church in a variety of capacities to grow and strengthen ministry in countless ways. During his travels to Dermott, Arkansas, he was introduced to Lizzie Woods, a matron of the Baptist Academy. She proved to be a woman of the highest social standard, maintaining outstanding stewardship in public service as an educator. Ms. Woods attended the National Convocation in Memphis, Tennessee where she accepted what is known within the denomination as the Doctrine of Pentecost. Manifesting his visionary leadership from God, Bishop Mason realized that God had revealed in this woman an organizer, motivator, and authentic leader. Lizzie Woods's God-given talents consequently paved the way for her being selected as the first general mother of women to organize and create work and projects that would be beneficial to women and the development of the church.

On her initial tour, she was introduced to her future spouse, Elder Robinson. Mother Lizzie Woods Robinson was appointed as Bishop Mason's counterpart. Under her guidance and leadership, the COGIC auxiliaries were developed which included the Bible Band, Sewing Circle, Home and Foreign Missions, Sunshine Band, and Purity Classes. The last two auxiliaries listed focused on the church's instruction for children and young female adults.

The purpose of the Sunshine Band was to train children between the ages of five and twelve on biblical principles and how to obey the Word of God so that their minds would not be destroyed by public elementary schools and broken homes. The Purity Class was specifically for young girls between the ages of twelve and sixteen to develop skills that would support healthful practices to grow happy and be moral adults. Mother Robinson taught the concepts of living by the Holy Bible utilizing domestic duties in the home, and encouraging young ladies to keep physically clean by bathing. Thus, the soul was cleansed by the Bible, the home cleansed by the broom, and the body cleansed by the bath.

Mother Robinson led these COGIC standards of morality and piety until her death, transitioning from labor to reward in 1945 while attending the annual COGIC Holy Convocation. Following her death, Lillian Brooks Coffey assumed leadership as national supervisor of the COGIC women's department, and completed Robinson's legacy by securing funds for electric signage to be placed over the national headquarters of the Church of God in Christ located in Memphis, Tennessee.

There is much that can be said about the strength that lies within a determined woman when properly supported by others who believe in her work and trust her guidance. There are also relevant points that attest to healthy mother-daughter relationships. One might indicate the significance of training and developing respect and empathy between two uniquely created individuals. Introduced within these pages is a mother-daughter relationship between the main character in this narrative Ella B. Agnew Gordon and her beloved mother, Honey. Placing emphasis on relationship building, we applaud mother-daughter leadership that naturally evolves as these two women created change and demonstrated leadership within the church built on the relationship they had with one another. "Like mother, like daughter" is not just a simple cliché when it becomes words that transcend into an uncomplicated meaning that sketches the outline of hardworking women.

Generational leadership among women also continues to remain a dominant force for growth and development of equity and diversity within today's church. For as long as work and kingdom building exists, there is room for a woman to accept the role and accomplish the task through the grace of God.

Chapter 1
Lineage and Legacy (Beginnings)

May the Lord make your love increase and overflow for each
other and for everyone else, just as ours does for you.
– 1 Thessalonians 3:12 (NIV)

THE DESCRIPTION OF a love affair and family values will become unearthed in the meaningful essence of humanity as Ella Belle tells her story of her parents' early childhood steeped in long suffering, agony, and affliction.

***

Ella's father, James, was born during seasonal picking time on a plantation where his mother died shortly after giving birth to him. His father was the White plantation owner who resided in Mobile, Alabama. Since there is limited knowledge of this man and of his factual where-abouts, we can only rely on generational folklore. His mother's best friend, also a migrant worker, promised to care for James and include him as part of her family; however, his formative years were void of care and subjected to daily abuse from his presumed caregiver.

James fell into a fiery pit of flames as a toddler, leaving him with severe burns. Over time, an unsightly scar began to protrude from the middle of his chest which caused him incredible despair. James never reviled his feelings about the appearance of the scar and how these scars emotionally left him. This was something that was never talked about in the family. And, we will never know the trauma he carried with him everyday.

It was only by the grace of God and a miracle that James survived and continued to thrive.

Paired with the mean streaks of anger and abuse from the woman raising James, he decided to run away from the only home he knew at an early age. James lived off the earth and secured odd jobs with different people as he moved around seeking better opportunities.

Gladys was Ella's mother. Her family background consisted of her older brother, Levi, and two older sisters, Lottie and Rubell Reed. Gladys' mother died when she was fourteen years old, leaving her father, Mose Reed, to provide a modest home life. Respectfully, Mr. Reed was a robust individual who ran his house with an iron fist. One thing was for sure, he did not approve of "holy rollers" (as he would label church people) from the Church of God in Christ where Gladys relished in worshipping. He would often refuse to allow Gladys to interact with members of that congregation and would punish her by not allowing her to attend services at the church.

His hard-nosed actions caused Gladys grief. So, she made sure that all of her chores were completed to the best of her abilities to ensure that her father would not have any fair-minded reason for her to not attend. The congregation members were quite aware of her father's disdain for the church and began to fervently pray for him to have a change of heart. They fasted and prayed until finally, he gave in and granted Gladys permission to join the church. This was the beginning of a new season in her life. A few years later, Mr. Reed passed away, leaving Gladys an orphan.

Neither James nor Gladys were beneficiaries of an extended family. Both of Ella's parents grew up not having any knowledge of family beyond parents. The portrait of this connection among two young people migrating to the North, separately and on their own, seeking a better lifestyle is the story of James Agnew and Gladys Reed. They were recruited as seasonal workers, commonly known as fruit-pickers, for harvesting. James migrated from Mobile, Alabama. Gladys traveled from Trenton, Tennessee. How they were transported to the State of Michigan where their seasonal work took place was unclear, but we do recognize that both looked forward to picking fruit during harvest time and had actually established a personal connection with each other. In an era where relationships were simple and far less complicated than that of today, these two relied on instinctive feelings to establish a courtship built on trust and hope.

James and Gladys were two young people attempting to create a better life with one another and for each other. At the end of the fruit-picking season, their affection was asserted with a mere handshake of agreement that proved to manifest a lasting legacy of love and commitment that was deep-rooted in a position of resilience.

"A tree cannot stand without roots." – Congolese Proverb

Chapter 2
Second Summer (Their Story)

Two are better than one; because they have a good reward for their
labour. For if they fall, the one will lift up his fellow: but woe to him
that is alone when he falleth; for he hath not another to help him up.
— Ecclesiastes 4:9-10 (KJV)

AS AN ONLY daughter, Ella Agnew engaged in conversations with reflections of her mother. She designated the endearing name "Honey" exclusively chosen for her dearest friend, role model, mentor, and family matriarch—Gladys.

***

The next summer, James and Honey returned to Michigan from their respective homes in the South. Their feelings for one another continued to develop. One could only imagine the depth of love and respect they must have felt by saving themselves as these young people were grounded in their spiritual beliefs and principles, established under the doctrines of the Church of God in Christ. Their second summer was a season that presented them with the chance to rekindle their abiding relationship, a silent love affair. As the harvest ended and the summer began to turn into fall, these seasonal fruit-pickers were united in marriage in August of 1935.

James and Honey Agnew started their family in Benton Harbor, Michigan with the birth of their oldest son, James, Jr., in 1936. Ella came in 1937, and their youngest, John, was born in 1939. James Agnew, Sr. was a short man in stature with very light-complected skin. An exceptional provider for his family and a well-respected businessman in the community, he was a self-taught man with a sixth grade education, and his vision of opening an industrial cleaning business resulted in the family moving to Michigan City, Indiana.

James and Honey Agnew

Shortly after the move, he developed a highly regarded relationship with Mr. and Mrs. Roderick. The Rodericks were White, highly esteemed, wealthy people of influence in the Agnews' new community. This association favored James with the ability to establish his own cleaning business in the early 1940s. In addition to the venture itself, the Rodericks were underwriters of his commercial contracts, which included banks and financial institutions, professional office buildings, and bowling allies and entertainment lounges. They also extended themselves by financing James' industrial cleaning equipment as part of the venture.

Ella adored her father and helped him in the business by accompanying him on cleaning trips. On many occasions when they cleaned lounges, she would often treat herself to an ice cream sundae or a delicious soda. She thoroughly delighted in the reward for this labor of love. Her impression of her father was one of a rich man as she observed the massive ring of keys that he wore, representing all of the companies that he provided services. Through Ella's eyes, those keys were symbolic of affluence and distinction from the ordinary. Her father had become a trusted, respected, and successful businessman. In her world, she was living large all because of her father's aspirations and forward-thinking mindset.

At the age of twelve, Ella found herself supportively assisting her father with bookkeeping and accounting responsibilities since her mother was not able to help upon the onset of what would become a debilitating illness, which will be focused more on later in this book. (Uncertain of her beloved mother's factual diagnosis, Ella indicated that it may have been rheumatoid arthritis.) Each week, Ella would accompany her father downtown to pay his weekly expenditures. She would stand in line and find herself frequently overlooked because of her height. People standing in line would signal to the clerk to look down as Ella was too short to reach the top of the counter, let alone be visible for clerks to see. Though small in stature, she was a grand asset and supporter to her father's business as she was able to proficiently learn the business (within seven facilities) and manage the accounts.

Young Ella was responsible for preparing company invoices and payroll for her father's employees. This was no easy undertaking, especially for a youth. Needless to say, her father was eternally thankful for her skillful aid in business as well as her dedication to the family.

When Honey wanted or needed something, she would tell Ella. In no time, her mother's requests would be fulfilled. It is relevant to note, while James was a great provider and impressive entrepreneur, it was difficult for him to express himself and expose his true feelings. Being the son of a plantation owner proved to be a devaluing reality and brought with it a loss of kinship. This disconnect never permitted him to establish a bond or relationship of any kind with his father. Best described as a kind of generic love where emotions lacked deep affection, nurturing feelings of any kinship was nearly nonexistent for him. Love was simply not in his footprint of lived experiences. There were no relatives to share in typical human kindnesses because there was no one. He was alone and lost in an unfamiliar search for natural emotions that he was just unable to identify. As a result of the abuse he endured early in his childhood, the task of communicating his feelings with warmth and compassion was void.

When it came to James's children, the relationship with his sons, James, Jr. and John, was strained, unlike the endearing relationship he had with Ella.

The dysfunctions of his early life experiences concerning his interpersonal interactions were quite challenging. While he loved his sons dearly, he did not show or express his feelings or desires because he had never learned what positive, engaging behaviors should resemble. Again, the heart that was robbed of true identity and self-validation in this world, stemming from the trauma of his early childhood, would remain the face that showed up when interacting more intimately with his family, particularly with his sons.

Ecstatic when she spoke of her relationship with her dear parents, Ella honestly believed theirs was a match made in heaven. James's love for his wife was in the form of protection and his duty as a provider. Their experience as migrant workers groomed him with an understanding of devotion and protection, and because of it, they were inseparable.

Pictured left to right James, Ella, and John Agnew

Both James and Honey were active members of the church and shared a deep respect for working in the church, as well. James was the head deacon working alongside another elder on the West Side of Michigan City. Honey was an active member of Hatchett Temple Church of God in Christ across the street from where Ella and her brothers grew up. Both parents were creating examples for their children to follow in their footsteps, on a path that fostered living a dedicated Christian lifestyle. James eventually acknowledged his calling into ministry.

The attributes of James Agnew, Sr.'s servant leadership came across as that of a quiet, unassuming man with an inherent affinity for his family and his workers. Consequently, in an era when racism and injustices were alive and well across the United States, this fair-complected man who exuded confidence and courage in his stride was able to walk into any restaurant, hotel, or public venue without being questioned. This was the Americanism that dates back to decades before his time, further initiating colorism which was one of the primary traits that led to his success. He was able to pass as a White man in the days when Jim Crow laws existed from the 1880s to the late 1960s. He would frequent White-owned establishments, specifically restaurants where he would order from menus and purchase food that his workers selected. He would then return with their selections to share for lunch while sitting with them on the back of their pickup trucks.

James's visionary competencies were sharp and unwavering. Using a mere limb of a broken tree branch, he sketched on bare earth a blueprint of what was to become his family's new home that he built on vacant land. With precision and skill, he continued to point out the scale of each room that he would design and designate its occupancy. Ella was elated and proud to learn that she would have her own bedroom. Her brothers shared a room and her parents shared a room, as well. Ella described this vision of her father as him building their mansion. There would be a breezeway connecting the house to the garage shielding the family from the natural elements. She was overjoyed with grand illusions associated with her classification of wealth, accomplishment, and respectability. In her mind, the Agnew's had arrived at a place of prestige and affluence.

Growing up in Michigan City, she and her brother James, Jr. were often assumed to be twins. Ella described their childhood relationship as being "joined at the hip" as they would walk together everywhere. When James moved to Durham, North Carolina, she intentionally left a pair of sneakers at his home with hopes of carrying on their strolls together as they shared memorable exchanges of their early childhood. Ella estimated that she and James walked three miles each day, along with enjoying the Sunday evening episodes of *60 Minutes* on television. Together, they would engage in long distance conversations, exchanging their opinions on the weekly current events. There would be no interruptions when these two enjoyed their weekly dialogue.

As life moves forward, Ella continues to savor conversations with her younger brother, John, that nourish the soul and keeps them close. John was actually reclaimed during one of her hosted spirit-filled prayer breakfasts, which will also be mentioned later. It was these very breakfasts that grew over time under her vision to serve as an arc for purposely bringing people together for fellowship, praise, and corporate prayer seeking God's heart.

Today, John respectfully serves as the oldest living deacon in the Greater Powerhouse Church of God in Christ in Indiana to this day. He is also the father of two daughters, Angela Agnew O'Dell and Dawn Agnew Taylor, grandfather of four, and great-grandfather of eight. Angela is the spouse of Van O'Dell who is employed as an information technologist. She is currently working in the healthcare industry in nursing as a healthcare manager. They are the proud parents of Tevan. Dawn and Larry Taylor have been married for five years and have a beautiful, blended family, being the parents of two daughters and three sons. Dawn is a member of the Spoken Word Church and serves in many capacities. This small family church often rotates positions, giving members an opportunity to serve God using their spiritual gifts in worship and service. Dawn is also in the healthcare field.

Ciara, John's oldest granddaughter, has followed in the footsteps of her mother and aunt by working in healthcare as a medical assistant. Jaime, now deceased, was a registered nurse and passed away in 2017. James is a quality control inspector. Jason has been married to Stephanie for thirteen years and is employed as a supervisor of security while his wife works as a receptionist. Breon works with youth and young adults as a self-defense instructor. Bringing up the rear of the Taylor family are eight grandchildren.

Insightful conversations with Ella's extended family also flourish. She spoke of Jerome, affectionately referred to as "J.J." Agnew. He is the only blood nephew of Ella Bell Agnew Gordon. Jerome is the son of James, Jr. and grandson of James, Sr. Recognizably, Jerome is the admirable role model for his family and community alike, as well as a living representation of his lineage as the only male—of his generation, as nephew of his Uncle John and Aunt Ella—to carry on as guardian of the Agnew family legacy. He has been married to Pandora Agnew for thirty-five years, a testament of an enduring relationship, and blessed to be proud parents of two daughters and two sons. His starting line-up consists of a home team which includes five grandchildren with anticipation of another new team member due to arrive in June 2023.

The Jerome Agnew family is steeped in military service to the United States, of which his country, family, friends, and fellow citizens are most grateful for. As a US Air Force retiree, having served his country for twenty-three years, Jerome continued employment in a civilian capacity for eighteen years with the US Department of Defense. His birthright has been the footing for a solid work ethic and foundation for achieving several academic degrees as a result of his scholarship and drive to succeed.

Indisputably attracted to a like-minded companion, Pandora is a retired certified nursing assistant having worked with military patients and various healthcare teams. Joseph, their oldest son, served in the United States Army for eight years and is pursuing a master's degree. Joseph's wife, Roxanne, has also served in the US Army. Pandora, named after her mother, is the oldest daughter and is currently an elementary school administrator. Her tenure as an educator has expanded over fourteen years. Needless to say, her scholarship and belief in the importance of having an education are invaluable. Pandora is married to Euvon and they have a child. Bridget is a substance abuse health educator and has established special interests in helping to promote positive youth growth and behavioral development among African American young adults. She is a candidate for an advanced degree in mental health in the spring of 2023.

The youngest of the Agnew children is Romeo who served in the United States Army. He is married to Jessica who is also a US Army veteran. It is reasonable to conclude that Ella's nephew trailed a similar path that parallels his paternal grandfather's drive, whether intentional or unplanned. It becomes apparent that Jerome's determination to provide and advance was the impetus for him and his helpmate to enhance their life and the lives of their family members.

As Ella went over the main points of her thoughts that came across as endearing reflections of her beloved parents and family, she appeared to be forever grateful and tremendously proud of her participation in the role that she manifested while supporting the family business— essentially, where it all began.

"If you want to know the end, look at the beginning." – African proverb

Chapter 3
Birth of a Woman (Herstory)

Train up a child in the way he should go:
and when he is old, he will not depart from it.
–Proverbs 22:6 (KJV)

GROWING UP IN Michigan City, Indiana proved to be a satisfying experience for Ella. She was able to establish meaningful, lasting relationships with her classmates and high school friends. Her best friends and playmates were twin sisters. The girls were on the soccer team and formed a tight bond. They attended the same high school and even spent their weekends together. Both families were intertwined and countless hours were spent with their mothers sharing goals and dreams they had for their daughters to grow and develop into outstanding educated women, along with being spiritually grounded in their faith. Ella's mother was particularly excited about her daughter's outstanding achievements and wanted to expose the girls to every promising opportunity possible.

Television was one connection for learning about opportunities that spanned beyond one's immediate community. Dr. Arenia Cornelia

Mallory, distinguished educator and headmaster of the Lexington Saints Industrial Finishing School in Lexington, Mississippi, under the auspices of the Church of God in Christ, came on national television as a guest speaker. *(For research purposes; it is relevant to note that with the expansion and reorganization of this private denominational school, it has been renamed several times, referred to also as Lexington Training School for Girls, Saints Junior College and Academy, and Saints Industrial and Literary School.)*

Among her acclaimed contributions, Dr. Mallory introduced a "sanctified dress code" intermingled with international garb. Conventional styles in fashion were representative of timelessness throughout history that served as a classic foundation for dress depicting sophistication and flair. Sanctification of the church was also influential in establishing this polished dress code for women that continues to be culturally dominant and prevalent in the current COGIC realm. Women would typically don tailored suits, stunning dresses, attention grabbing hats with an array of textures, and accessories from stockings and church gloves to fancy furs with attire that modeled styles of dress of women in the United Kingdom, Canada, Australia, New Zealand, Jamaica, Barbados, Grenada, New Guinea, the Solomon Islands, Tuvalu, Saint Lucia, other parts of the Caribbean, and countries associated with the commonwealth.

As Ella and her friends listened intently to Dr. Mallory's address, Ella found herself becoming deeply attracted to this motivational message. Following Dr. Mallory's presentation, Ella told her mother that she would very much like to attend the Lexington Saints Industrial Finishing School.

Ella and her mother returned to their church to express Ella's desire to enroll in the school. With the support of the mothers of the church,

Honey started working painstakingly as she took on any opportunity that she could to earn money for Ella to attend. She would scrub floors, bake homemade cakes and pies, and churn handmade ice cream until they were able to save enough for Ella's tuition.

Ella's indoctrination and influence, relative to the COGIC culture, had exposed her to discipline and order. Her Sundays alone were filled with regulation and decorum as part of her church-going routine. Church bells would ring out early in the morning as a call to assemble for Sunday services. For Sunday school children, it was a must to enter the church in a straight line, almost resembling little tin soldiers, respectfully and well-behaved. The rules of the Church of God in Christ were strict, making children aware that there was no running, talking, or chewing gum in church. Girls were prohibited from crossing their legs, and eye contact was not allowed. A child's focus was meant to be looking straight ahead. Needless to say, Ella was able to take these lessons with her upon being accepted to the Lexington Industrial Finishing School.

During her experience at Lexington, Ella had the opportunity to join the school choir which traveled across the country. Modeling after the Jubilee Singers of Fisk University, students not only had an opportunity to serve, but to see another world outside of their personal lens that was quite different from the harsh conditions growing up in the Jim Crow South. Singing in the choir provided Ella and other students with a new world vision of church life as well as engagement with other youth groups outside of the COGIC faith, along with an introduction to the reality of new ideology.

Ella's relationship with Dr. Mallory allowed her to reside in the best homes belonging to prominent leaders that included presidents of other colleges and bishops of the church as the choir toured throughout the country. While she was exposed to fine living and proper etiquette, other choir members were residing in the homes of church members since Blacks were not allowed to stay in commercial hotels. At the time, slavery had been eradicated, but Jim Crow laws remained prevalent. For Ella, the school was evidence of an immense, life-changing realization; an epiphany that shaped her future and favored her with an extraordinary outcome of her young adult life and work experiences along the way.

She graduated in May of 1955 and returned home to Michigan City. Ella was employed as a receptionist during the day with the only African American physician in town while attending evening classes at South Bend College of Commerce.

While back home, Ella met Hattie White, an alumna of Elton High School and a good friend of her mother's. In June of 1957, Mrs. White—accompanied by her husband and two children—traveled back to Michigan City for her twenty-fifth class reunion. The Whites attended church on Sunday morning where they were introduced to Honey's daughter, Ella Agnew. This initial introduction between two daughters was the start of over six decades of a sister-friend relationship between Ella and Hattie's daughter, Doris. (As of 2022, these spirited ladies were roommates at the 114th Holy Convocation held in Memphis, Tennessee.)

Over time, the mothers rekindled their friendship and Ella was allowed to visit with Mrs. White and her children in Detroit, Michigan. During the visits, Ella was able to apply for and take civil service exams. When her results were received with high scores, she was able to acquire employment with the Michigan State Employment Security Commission.

Ella and Doris had become close friends by this time. These two young women would often attend church together at State Temple

Church of God in Christ in Detroit. Doris was the reason Ella met Wilder Lee "Bo" Gordon, who she would be engaged to the following year. In December of 1958, Bo and Ella had an elegant candlelight wedding in Michigan City at Hatchet Temple Church of God in Christ. Doris was Ella's maid of honor, and Bo's two friends and Ella's brothers made up the wedding party. The newly wedded couple returned to Detroit that same evening. They resided with Bo's parents for one year, then moved into their own home.

On August 18, 1964, their son Leslie Lamont Gordon was born. His parents lovingly nicknamed him "Monty." As life shifted in an unfamiliar direction, Ella and Bo divorced in 1975, leaving her to raise "Monty," her only child, as a single mother. She and "Monty" became each other's biggest supporters.

Monty followed in his mother's footsteps by graduating from the Lexington School in Mississippi. He continued his education by attending and graduating from Oral Roberts University, a Christian University in Tulsa, Oklahoma. Monty's hidden talent surfaced as a creative writer and his love of poetry. God gifted Monty with expressing his true meaning of life through the written word. As an example of his creative writing, Monty penned "The Light of My Life: A Tribute to My Mother on her 80th Birthday." He wrote…

Pictured Ella and Young "Monty"

"The first command of God rendered in the Bible can usually be remembered by virtually anyone, Christian or not. Theologians speculate as to which part of the Godhead actually spoke the first words recorded in the Bible—the Father, the Son, or the Holy Spirit–but in this setting, it makes no difference because I say this only to show the importance of this thing that we call Light.

God didn't need Light, for His Glory is enough to light the universe, so why did He create it FIRST? I believe He initiated it for the sake of the apex of His creation, man. God wanted man to be able to see that which was before him so that he could make informed, intelligent and correct choices. But why am I telling you this? Why am I saying this at a celebration of my dear mother's 80th birthday? I'm glad you asked!

When I thought of all the wonderful things that my mother has done in my life while raising me, teaching me, and guiding me, I stumbled onto something that I had never noticed before: the meaning of my mother's name.

Her middle name, Belle, of course, means 'beautiful' especially in the French language, but I had never researched the name Ella. I always thought it was short for something else and left it at that, but I was wrong. The name Ella literally means 'Light.' I don't know if my sainted grandmother knew that she had christened her daughter as 'beautiful light' or not, but no other name could have fit her nature more exactly.

Most of you in this room have known my mother for many years and if you have, then you know how well this appellation fits her personality, her nature, and the way she affects the world around her. When Ella walks into a room, it does, indeed, brighten as if someone had literally turned on a light. When Ella speaks and imparts information, the light of knowledge and wisdom enters into the minds and hearts of those who hear her words. When Ella smiles, one's day lights up with joy.

Is she perfect? No, for only God is perfect, but she strives for perfection in all she does. She presses for excellence in herself and tries to aid all those around her to be as excellent and perfect as Jesus is, for this is her own goal as she goes through life.

How do I know this? I have seen it all my life. I am proud to say that I am her only begotten son and my mother, my Ella has been my Light since before I knew what Light was. The scripture says: 'Arise, shine; for thy light is come, and the glory of the LORD is risen upon thee (Isaiah 60:1 KJV).' The scripture from the Book of Isaiah, of course, refers to the coming of Christ the Messiah, but when I see this passage, I imagine it was spoken to me as I emerged from my mother's womb and was born into this world, as a reassurance that I would have my mother's light in my life to show me to the path of knowledge, to guide me and to enlighten me; to expose me to many diverse cultures and cuisines such as Middle Eastern, Mediterranean, Caribbean, Korean, and African; to bring me the wisdom of times past by taking me to museums and introducing me to friends and acquaintances who knew more by experience than even she did.

She cast the light of God's Word before me by purchasing Bible storybooks and record sets for me when I was a child, taking me to church, having me spend my summer with my grandmother, Mother Gladys "Honey" Agnew, and by introducing me to powerful and knowledgeable men and women of God, so that I would have other examples of holy living besides her own.

My mother, my Ella, my Light – showed me other religions as well as Christianity not so I would think to have a choice, but so that I would see that Christ Jesus is the ONLY WAY to eternal salvation and temporal shalom (the peace of having nothing missing and nothing broken in life)! For Allah did not give his own life to save anyone as Jesus did to save the world and Buddha provides no healing for the body or the mind through his name as the name of Jesus does! But most of all, there is no other sacrifice that is accepted by our Creator and Heavenly Father as is the blood of the innocent Christ on the cross for our sins that provides a way for us to be reconciled for Him!

This is the way that my mother, my Ella, my Light that God placed in my life led me; this is what I can never possibly ever give enough gratitude for as the scripture says: 'The spirit of man is the lamp of the LORD; searching all the innermost parts of his being' (Proverbs 20:27 NASB). The way my mother led me to the Lord, allowed me to know of and seek the Lord's gift of the Holy Ghost, whose inward, indwelling presence ignited my spirit and searches me deep inside to this day, so I can let my light shine and obey the Lord Jesus's commandment: 'Let your light so shine before men, that they may see your good works, and glorify your Father which is in heaven.' (Matthew 5:16 KJV)

Thank You seems a poor and inadequate way to express my appreciation for all that my mother, my Ella, my Light has done for me, and so I use the gift that the Lord has expressed through me that began at such a young age, the gift of words. I hope in some small way that this tribute to my mother, my Ella, my Light can bring out and truly express my gratitude and my pride at being her only begotten son and let her know how much I deeply and truly love her...now and forevermore...that she is and will always be the Light of my life.'"

Monty became a columnist for the *LaPorte County Herald Dispatch* where he submitted several articles. More importantly, though (Ella was uncertain of the exact date), she remembered when Monty dedicated his life to the ministry. Monty was married for twenty-two years to his wife, Cheryl. Ella's dear son was diagnosed with a kidney disorder which resulted in fifteen years of dialysis treatments. His health continued to decline which led to his death on February 2, 2018.

Her career continued to advance as she was hired with the Federal Government during former President Ronald Reagan's administration. Shortly thereafter, President Reagan upgraded the stipulations for federal retirement where employees serving twenty-five years would become eligible for retirement regardless of age restriction. In April 1987, Ella was happily able to retire at the age of forty-nine. A retirement dinner was held in her honor at the exclusive Rooster Tail Supper Club in Detroit, Michigan. While there, Ella proudly showcased the opening of Honey's Boutique (specializing in fashions that celebrated clothing first ladies of the church). In honor of

Monty High School Graduation

her mother, Honey's Boutique became her second launch into the business world. Reflecting on her early life experiences, specifically working with her father in the cleaning industry and her mother in fundraising by seeking financial support for the church and other charities, Ella B. Gordon had indisputably been bitten by the entrepreneurial bug. She was excited about another new beginning.

Combined with her business skills and forward-thinking vision, she was able to develop unique fashions exclusively designed to suit each woman's individual style. Her effective listening skills would serve her well as a key trait in creating an atmosphere where each of her clients felt listened to, particularly when communicating their specific needs, and by establishing a one-of-a-kind portfolio that was exclusively theirs. This project led Ella to an international business community which propelled her into worldwide commerce.

As an entrepreneur, Ella traveled to the International Designer Show in Milan, Italy, then to the Leather International Designer Show in Offenbach, Germany. The business also extended her travels to Istanbul, Paris, Seoul, and Hong Kong. Because of the favor of God and the partnership turned friendship with Mr. and Mrs. Kanar, Ella was able to travel to Istanbul, Turkey on four separate occasions. As a result of this special relationship, the Kanars opened their homes by providing Ella with her own suite in Istanbul as well as a room in their Florida home.

After opening Honey's Boutique, Ella was hired with Northwest Airlines Corporation (a major United States airline that existed until 2010 when it merged with Delta Air Lines, Inc.). When she learned there were employment opportunities at Delta Air Lines as an airport customer service representative, she pursued it. Following her interview, this savvy sixty-five-year-old senior was hired on site. Ella's entrepreneurship and establishment of Honey's Boutique would symbolize over two decades of hard work, commitment, and dedication invested in the Metro-Detroit region until 2012.

Having accomplished the goal of providing high quality service to first ladies of the church across a wide range of denominations to include entertainers and women in leadership, her business venture generated over two decades of incredible success. The boutique fostered relationships that extended to profitable joint business ventures which afforded the comforts of an extraordinary lifestyle. The knowledge she acquired from her beloved parents in business was part of the fabric that clothed her with preparedness defining her as a strong, independent woman. Preparedness, however, would become a relative term when the harsh realities of life showed up in a pretentious world.

Monty and Ella

"Knowledge is a garden. If it is not cultivated, you cannot harvest it."
–Ovambo Proverb

Chapter 4
Life With Its Challenges and Changes

All Scripture is God-breathed and is useful for teaching,
rebuking, correcting and training in righteousness...
–2 Timothy 3:16 (NIV)

FOR YEARS, HONEY'S health declined. Ella was accustomed to supporting and assisting her mother as her primary caregiver. In reality, though, she was not prepared to accept the harsh reality of her mother's demise. Both parents, James and Honey, were faced with deteriorating health, which required frequent medical attention. In April of 1980, Gladys "Honey" Reed Agnew passed away. The woman who led by her life example for Ella to emulate would suffer no more.

Restricted to a wheelchair to support his mobility, James was able to attend the funeral service of his dear wife. The once provider and protector lived with a diagnosis of chronic diabetes. Physicians were scheduling him for an elective procedure which would involve surgical amputation of an undetermined number of his toes. Through steadfast prayer, James continued to mentally prepare himself for surgery while, at the same time, tried to emotionally come to grips with the loss of his true love and their family's matriarch.

His surgery was set for the Monday that followed his wife's burial; a mere four days later. Sadly, James Agnew died at 5:30 that Monday morning, just three hours before his procedure was to take place. When Ella arrived at the hospital one final time on her father's behalf, she actually provided comfort to his physician as he greeted her visibly devastated at the loss of his patient. With resolve, she expressed to him that her father did it his way. "Since this was his appointed day of death, better he died at 5:30 a.m. than at 8:30 a.m. under your scalpel," she said.

Being a proud man who wrestled with showing his genuine feelings, he did not want to become dependent on anyone else to take care of him. She continued posing questions and disclosing her beliefs, saying to her father's physician, "What if he had expired during surgery? How would you have been able to cope with the loss of your patient? Doc, you really weren't aware of my parents' love for one another." It seemed as if James no longer wanted to live a sorrowful life absent of many things through loss. The love of his life had been diminished and the realities of living without her became glaring and not something that he wanted to bear.

Even in Ella's own grief, she was able to advise and console her father's physician as if she were the professional counseling on death and comforting in times of despair. Deeply touched by her assessment as this humble professional exposed a side that was seldom displayed for grieving families to witness, the physician wanted to be present during the family's time of bereavement. He thought it would be fitting to invite Ella and her two brothers to his home to share a meal and spend a few moments together during their mutual loss.

Again, Ella Gordon found herself in preparation for another funeral. Layers of grief and loss kept surfacing as these real life nightmares seemed to spiral. Outfitted in mental exhaustion and overwhelmed with anguish and sorrow, her present state was the introduction of Ella's unforeseeable future when she would reach out to the man who she considered to be the love of her life to inform him of her father's death.

Longing for some psychological freedom to escape her sadness; Ella, unassumingly, contacted her companion of several years hoping to engage in an early morning chat. However, much to her chagrin, she was greeted by an unfamiliar voice answering his phone. The woman on the other end of her lover's extension responded in a languid voice stating that he had already left for work, but she would kindly give him the message. Ella described the pain as being hit in the gut, leaving her breathless and sucker punched with disbelief. How on earth could this be! Already heartbroken with the loss of her mother and her father, she was mortified to learn that she had actually lost what she thought was the man of her dreams.

This man was capable of publicly displaying conciliatory support by attending the services of both parents; however, by that point, their relationship would face an abrupt ending. The traumatic experiences that accompanied death, loss, and betrayal forced Ella to look introspectively at her life and figure things out to regain her shine in response to the life-changing events that resulted in her losing her luster.

Recapturing her focus supported by more sustainable professional and social paths enabled Ella to discover that she was living an exuberant lifestyle, leaving her spirituality unprotected. This epiphany was beyond insightful causing her to undeniably realize that she had selfishly attributed her achievements being hardworking and self-made, instead of acknowledging her successes were because of the goodness of God and His covering over her life. In all of her successes, Ella realized that she had distanced and separated herself from God and her covering, the church. In doing so, she acknowledged that she had lived a lifestyle that facilitated her backsliding. While she never stopped going to church, Ella would arrive at church late and leave out early. She had convinced herself that she was able to succeed outside of the ark of God's covenant.

Her initial reflection was an acknowledgment of her spiritual separation in unorthodox relationship. She was spiritually aware that she was participating in a relationship considered to be unmentionable by craving intimacy with someone outside of the church and outside of marriage.

In her quest to fix a broken situation, Ella sought spiritual redemption by faithfully attending Tuesday morning prayer. One of the church mothers took time to provide words of encouragement and offered affirmations of God's forgiveness. Thirteen years of backsliding could have proven to be a destructive lifestyle, but by the grace of God, Ella Gordon was afforded a second chance for redemption. One Tuesday morning during a regular prayer service, Ella was reclaimed. At that moment, she began running around the church with melodic outbursts singing, "I'm free! Praise the Lord, I'm free! No longer bound, no more chains holding me. My soul is resting, and it's just a blessing. Praise the Lord, hallelujah! I'm free. I'm free! Praise the Lord, I'm free! I've been saved and sanctified, filled with His holiness. I'm resting. It's another blessing! Praise the Lord! Hallelujah! I'm free."

Tearfully, Ella explained that it felt as if a weight had been lifted and that she was feeling as light as a bird flying high in the sky. This was an extremely emotional dialogue as Ella cried out, "If you don't have God in your life, you are carrying a death sentence." Notwithstanding the loss of her parents and her lover, life without God would be the worst possible experience ever lived and she spoke of it. After composing herself, Ella defined that Tuesday morning experience as her testimony. She has continued to walk in faith following God's lead since that time. Her spiritual transformation gave way to a new beginning of optimism and light in her life. This helped redefine her Christian path as she gained clearer perspective of living for the Lord.

It is relevant to mention three principles of faith that Ella Gordon's pastor outlines in his messages, which are identified as Ella's spiritually healthy practices. These emergent themes have become her actuality:

1) You must see it. Visualize your faith.

2) You must say it. Speak your faith into existence.

3) You must claim it. Own the physical reality of your faith.

–J. D. S.

"He who refused to obey cannot command." – Kenyan Proverb

Chapter 5

Redeeming Grace,
Picking Up the Pieces

Remain in me, as I also remain in you. No branch can bear fruit by itself; it must remain in the vine. Neither can bear fruit unless you remain in me. —John 15:4 (NIV)

ELLA'S VOYAGE INTO the new millennium continued to reign with success through God's anointing; however, she was not exempt from sickness, trials, or suffering. Ella Gordon came across two points in her life when she was diagnosed with breast cancer and COVID-19.

***

The racial disparity in deaths from cancer has remained at 40 percent or higher for a decade. African American women younger than fifty had a death rate twice as high as White women of the same age. African American women diagnosed with breast cancer continue to have the highest mortality rates in our present society. Although the mortality rate for breast cancer has been declining, a racial disparity continues to persist within the Black community.

In addition to breast cancer, African American women are now faced with being placed at a higher risk of contracting and dying from COVID-19. African American women with secondary diagnosis such as heart disease, asthma, obesity, and diabetes are prevalent among breast cancer patients so that if COVID-19 was contracted, the outcome would likely result in death.

Breast cancer has become the primary diagnosis of 12 percent of women residing in the United States. Over the course of their lifetime, more than 250,000 new cases of breast cancer were diagnosed in the United States in 2017. In layman's terms, breast cancer has been categorized into three major subtypes based on the presence or absence of molecular markers for estrogen or progesterone receptors and human epidermal growth (ERBB2; formerly HER 2): hormone receptor positive ERBB2 negative (70 percent of patients), ERBB2 positive (15 to 20 percent), and triple negative tumors (lacking all three standard molecular markers; 15 percent).

More than 90 percent of breast cancers are non-metastatic at the time of diagnosis. Patients with ERBB2 positive tumors receive antibody or small-molecule inhibitor therapy combined with chemotherapy. Triple-negative tumors receive chemotherapy alone. Local therapy for all patients with non-metastatic breast cancer consists of surgical resection, with consideration of post-operative radiation if lumpectomy is performed.2

In April of 2002, Ella was diagnosed with breast cancer. Her breast cancer treatment included the removal of her right breast, followed by six months of chemotherapy. Thirteen years later, in January of 2015, Ella was diagnosed with breast cancer in her left breast. The treatment modality involved the removal of this breast. As a result of an early diagnosis, there were no additional treatments required (Praise God!). After a few years of receiving a clean bill of health, Ella was faced with something completely unforeseen in March of 2020 as she was diagnosed with COVID-19.

In spite of recurring health challenges, invasive medical procedures, and various treatments (some more promising than others), Ella Gordon continued to press on with determination and conviction. Particularly when the doors of the church flew open, she wanted to be right there as usual. Her church life was the life that enveloped her with hope. She would start preparing for church early in the morning. Part of her ritual was making sure she looked better than up-to-par by always making it a point to look good because it made her feel better, especially when attending Sunday service. With a "beat face," her makeup would be flawless, a portrait of perfection. And with that same energy, this faithful servant wholeheartedly praised God for selecting her to endure multiple tests of faith. She felt as though God had enough confidence in her to withstand any test put before her, and that she would pass these examinations with triumphant praises of joy.

Ella wholeheartedly believes that she is a living testimony and to accept with joy what God allows. This was the emergent theme that dominated her life experiences since 2002. Fascinatingly, Ella went on to explain in our conversations that the Lord was her strength and her song. She would find joy and gain courage from listening and singing gospel music, along with reading scriptures from the Holy Bible, which became her emotional antidote in overcoming breast cancer and COVID-19.

I would be remiss if I did not disclose facts about breast cancer being a significant health problem among African American women.

Since the church is a visible health education venue serving as a point of community outreach, communicating with others about cancer prevention and spiritual care for cancer patients are critical areas of consideration that should promote inclusive cancer awareness. Various researchers and agencies, along with volunteer organizations have developed spiritually-based breast cancer education booklets that are distinctively intended for African American women. It is believed that this approach may be one way to make cancer communication more culturally appropriate for African American women.

Researchers have described breast cancer as an important area to target efforts toward eliminating health disparities. Although White women have higher breast cancer incidences compared to African American women (113.2 vs. 99.3 per 100,000 women respectively), the mortality rate for African American women is higher than that for White women (31.4 vs. 25.7 per 100,000 respectively). African American women are more likely than White women to die of breast cancer because their cancer, on average, is diagnosed at a later stage.[3]

Spirituality has played a culturally relevant role in the lives of many African Americans; mainly, African American women of an older age who are more religiously involved in the church than other populations. Attending church is far more than the practice of showing up and sitting on a pew. Church services provide African American women with social support. There is a legacy in the Black church that extends from the pulpit to the pews where congregants form relationships that endure generations. Prayer has historically been the heart of it all when acknowledging and calling upon a higher power. It is believed that a healthy prayer life strengthens one's ability to cope with stresses of life. As expected, prayer has been the foundation of Ella's faith and that of her family alike.

The following recommendations for self-care were included in an educational booklet for African American Women:

> ➤ Women should perform monthly breast self-examinations.
> ➤ Women should be aware of their family history of breast cancer.
> ➤ Pain associated with a mammogram is more like a discomfort, and it lasts only a short time. The result outweighs the discomfort.
> ➤ Women should talk to the doctor during general check-ups or wellness examinations.
> ➤ Most breast lumps are not cancerous.
> ➤ Women age 40 and over need to have annual mammograms for the rest of their lives, not just once.[4]

Coronavirus disease (COVID-19) has a societal affect comparable only to the Spanish flu epidemic of 1918. More is being learned about which individuals and groups experience the most dreadful complications. Researchers emphasized older age, hypertension, and heart disease were contributing factors to the coronavirus pandemic. In the earlier days of the pandemic, African Americans in Michigan represented four of every ten COVID-19 deaths; a startling number given they make up 14 percent of the state's population. This unfortunate trend took advantage of health disparities affecting communities of color. Blacks were more likely to suffer from heart disease, diabetes, obesity, and other ailments that made them more susceptible to COVID-19. Families were losing brothers, sisters, husbands, wives, cousins, teachers, ministers, students, and grandparents.[5]

On March 2, 2020, Ms. Gordon was invited to a good friend's eightieth birthday celebration. While attending, everyone sitting at her table of ten contracted COVID-19 with one exception. Several were hospitalized, one person died, and Ella remained in isolation at her home for nearly six weeks. During that time, she talked about being alone and extremely weaken by the disease, unable to prepare meals for herself and maintain her routine activities of daily living. The members of the church would prepare home-cooked meals and include fresh fruit to nourish her body each day, placing complete meals on a chair located outside her door. Being older, and unvaccinated at the time, she was considered to be a high risk patient if she were hospitalized, though she suffered through while under quarantine at home.

The odds of her survival remained limited. In spite of the virus and all the little known facts that severely impacted people all across the globe, the faithful members of her church continued to fast and pray without ceasing for her recovery. When I inquired about her faith and her reliance on God's healing powers during her gradual recovery as a result of contracting COVID-19, Ms. Ella smiled and whispered, "By the grace of God, I'm still here."

"You have little power over what's not yours."
– Zimbabwean Proverb

Chapter 6

He Keeps On Making a Way

In everything give thanks: for this is the will of God
in Christ Jesus concerning you.
-1 Thessalonians 5:18 (KJV)

THE HISTORY OF what we refer to as a "prayer breakfast" started in the 1930s with Vereide who found work as an itinerant Methodist Minister. He served as director of Goodwill Industries in Seattle and spent the first part of his career doing relief work for the poor and needy during the Great Depression. In April 1935, Vereide's prayers yielded what he claimed was a vision and plan revealed to him late in the midnight hour. Later that month, he gathered nineteen local businessmen for the first Seattle prayer breakfast.[6] Twenty-three years later, Ella Gordon—like Abraham Vereide—also shared God's vision in the creation of a prayer breakfast for women. Ella made it clear to me that this prayer breakfast project was a vision from God. His vision included two directives. First, Ella was to use her receipt book containing her entire clientele from Honey's Boutique to formulate the initial Prayer Breakfast Project. Secondly, revenue from this project included the sale of tables from her client base. With these two mandates from God, Ella moved forward to promote His vision. She unequivocally stated, "It was not of my own doing, or my idea. I was led by God."

Ella was chairperson of the twenty-fifth annual Women's Day Program, which was founded by the late Mother Annie Lee Bailey (first lady of the prominent Bailey Temple Church of God in Christ). This event was held on the second Sunday in February annually. Mother Bailey established Women's Day to help defray costs of the church's heating expenses during the winter months. During that time, Ella served as coordinator of the prayer breakfast and brunch which was established in February 1991. Her vision consisted of forming a group of women to include first ladies of local church organizations, entertainers, politicians, and women in business. These women were requested to purchase one table which included ten tickets.

In addition to supplementing the heat expenses of the church, this group of women provided a stable infrastructure for the Bailey Temple Church of God in Christ in Detroit, Michigan. Ella realized that these Saturday morning breakfast meetings—centered on prayer, Bible study, and creating powerful and profitable relationships among female leaders—would soon become a futuristic approach to God's vision and her success as a leader. Ella's method of reaching out to women in the community proved to manifest an influential Christian base and non-denominational network of stakeholders that helped advance the Bailey Temple Church of God in Christ for two decades of fundraising and joint ventures. The church was able to transform their kitchen through a reconstruction project consisting of an industrial, state of the arts facility.

Timing is everything in planning, and because the breakfast was slated for Saturday followed by the Sunday morning Women's Day program, Ella started planning at least six months prior to the event for the much anticipated breakfast. In December, she even designed centerpieces in red and white as Valentine's Day was readily approaching and near to that date. First ladies, along with their guests, came donned in scarlet. It is apparent that more emergent themes of love, friendship, and sisterhood were visible.

During our conversation, Ella continued to share how early prayer breakfast programs were designed. The program would usually consist of two prayers prior to hearing from a guest speaker and a prayer would conclude morning breakfast. The standard was to always feature an opportunity for personal testimonies and celebration in song. It was established that the breakfast guest speaker would also serve as the speaker for the Women's Day Celebration, often giving participants a sneak preview of what was to come on Sunday morning. This was also a marketing technique for sharing inspirational feedback to welcome other guests that had not planned to attend.

While we chatted, Ms. Ella smiled, allowing her imagination to recapture memories of Evangelist Jackie McCullough when she served as guest speaker—leading the women in prayer with her grace and elegance. Evangelist McCullough acknowledged, "Even in the worst of times, there is something to be thankful for: Thank Him that your faith has not dwindled. Thank Him that you're not hanging your head down in hopelessness. Thank Him that no matter what goes on, you still know that the Lord is with you. Thank Him for the blood running through your veins. As long as He is on the throne, things can get better. So make it praise from a thankful heart." Spontaneous eruptions of spirited emotions were heard, shouting aloud, "Hallelujah! Praise the Lord!" These shouts resonated throughout the church that culminated a highly charged gathering with singing and spiritual dancing. These women were exuberant when praising the Lord. Oh, what a time they had!

Ella went on to recall the transformational experience of her younger brother, John. He had been backsliding from the church for over four decades. While traveling by bus, John was accompanying the choir members from Gary, Indiana and East Chicago, Illinois to Detroit as featured gospel entertainment for the prayer breakfast. Evangelist McCullough's rousing sermon that was inarguably filled with the Holy Ghost did it! The bus ride home was inundated with ongoing praise and worship as the choir members and John relished in the Holy Spirit by glorifying the Lord. It was an emotional time as life came full circle for John and he was reunited with the church in April of 1997. He remains an active member to this day.

The original prayer breakfast coordinated by Ella Gordon was held in the basement of Bailey Temple Church of God in Christ. The growth that took place by God's vision continued to increase and its popularity did, as well. The prayer breakfast moved to four different locations throughout Michigan, which included Fair Lane Grand Manor in Dearborn, the Hyatt Regency Hotel, the river-view level of Cobo Hall; and, finally expanded to the main floor of Cobo Hall (currently known as the Huntington Place) in Detroit, Michigan. Indisputably, Ella's success model, from prayer breakfasts to prayerful feasts, could be summarized as an unhindered spirit of giving. She was giving in devotion. She was giving of her love. And she was giving in delight.

For over two decades of elevation, from planning prayer breakfasts at Bailey Temple in the basement to prayerful feasts on the main level of the renowned Cobo Hall, doors were opened to fulfill God's design.

"When one door closes another opens." – African Proverb

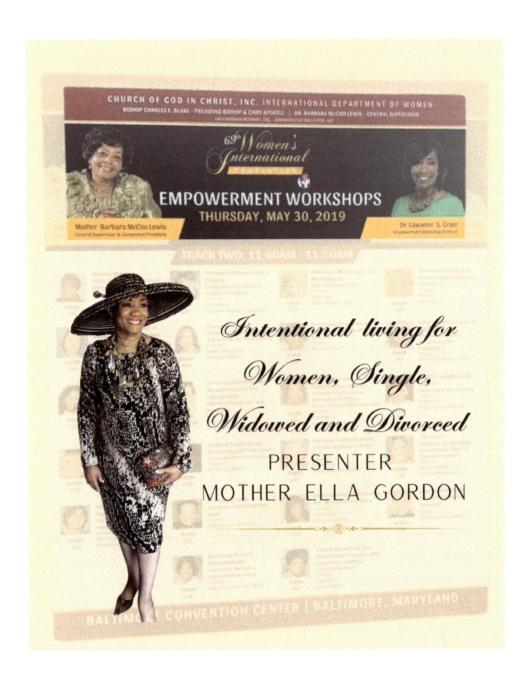

Chapter 7

Mosaics of Ella Belle Agnew Gordon's Impact

But he who is greatest among you shall be your servant.
-Matthew 23:11 (NKJV)

ELLA

"A LADY OF ELEGANCE"

Goddaughter Sonja Ison Simpsonville, SC

AS A YOUNG child, I noticed a very well-dressed lady who attended my church. She was the picture of elegance. Her hair was perfectly sculpted when she wasn't wearing a hat. Her clothes were always unique and her accessories were equally as exquisite as her outfits. Her shoes and purse always matched every outfit and her hats were well coordinated, too. Everything was always accessorized with just the right jewelry rendering her a picture of beauty. And, finally, there were her coats, which completed the look of elegance.

I watched this lady Sunday after Sunday and marveled at her appearance, but this was not the only attribute that caught my attention. This lady of elegance possessed a unique demeanor. I was in awe at the way she handled herself, especially when you knew she was not pleased. She would maintain her calmness in various situations while managing to keep a smile. I truly admired this quality and wondered how she could stay so cool even when she might have been dissatisfied.

I knew this lady was a friend of my mother's; however, I was always taught a child should stay in their place, so I was careful to not overstep my boundaries. But one day, I found the nerve to tell her how much I admired the way she dressed and that I wished to grow up and dress like her. She smiled and thanked me for the compliment. I then asked, "If you ever feel the need to clean-out your closet, I would be delighted to be the recipient of those items." She smiled and said, "I would be delighted to give you some things." She then asked me, "What size do you wear?" I remembered feeling a wealth of emotions; relieved that she was open to my request, and excited to see what outfit she would choose to bless me with. To this day, Ella is still turning heads when she enters the room.

I recall an outfit she gave me. It was a beautiful, well-tailored, black and red suit with a folded back red lapel and a black flared skirt that tapered at the waist. I felt so elegant when I wore that outfit. It was as if I was channeling her aura. It wasn't long after that I asked her if she would be my godmother. She replied, "Yes!" From that day forward, our loving relationship began and continues to flourish.

Throughout my life, I have admired the skills, talents, accomplishments, tenacity, and faith this woman has exhibited in overcoming the trials and tribulations of life. Though I was blessed to be the child of a God-fearing woman who possessed many skills, talents, and gifts that she nurtured in me, God also blessed me with a godmother who possessed similar characteristics. My mother approved and encouraged me to develop a loving relationship with her friend and my self-appointed godmother, Ella B. Gordon.

As I got to know and become closer to my godmother, I discovered we shared a lot of common threads. Not only did we both like to be well-dressed, but we often purchased the same shoes. We wore the same shoe size and sometimes the same clothing size. She likes to decorate. So do I. She is a singer. So am I. She likes to travel around the world, and so do I. The list became endless of many things we both enjoyed together—even without knowing. It was as if God knew I was the daughter she was meant to have. It was once stated by Monty, her beloved son, that he would sometimes confuse me with her when entering the church. He said that he thought I was more like her daughter sometimes than he was like her son.

I could go on and on talking about shared moments in anticipation of more to come. However, I will end these reflections with this: I am blessed to have a God-fearing woman like Ella in my life and to claim her as my godmother. She has encouraged me in a multitude of ways, and she recognized the opportunity to enhance my life. Though my biological mother has gone to her heavenly home, I know I still have an earthly godmother who loves me and continues to pray for me that I can talk to when I need godly advice. For this, I thank God!

Ella

"Inspiration and Grace"

Sentiments from Bishop Gregory G. M. &
Rev. Dr. Jessica Kendall Ingram, West Bloomfield, MI

I met Ella in 1987 when my husband, Gregory G. M. Ingram, and I moved to Detroit. My husband's cousin introduced me to Ella. There was an immediate connection. You would often find me in the basement at Honey's Boutique purchasing clothes. Sometimes if it was just for one event, I even rented clothes. We have spent time together at different church events and conferences; however, I never knew her history or background. I just knew she was somebody special in Detroit and in the Church of God in Christ. Reading about her family has given me much insight. Knowing some of her life story has given me a deeper respect for her. Ella is a woman who—once she makes up her mind—is unstoppable! This kind of determination has been a source of inspiration for me.

Ella and I are ten years apart. My birthday is July 25 and hers is August 25. I will turn seventy-six this year and she will be eighty-six. When I read her story, I connected with her retiring at forty-nine from her job, and making the pivot to start a successful business. As one who just recently retired, and who has taken on a new God-given ministry, Ella is Exhibit number one in demonstrating what a made up mind can do. Once God gave her the vision for business, she moved forward and didn't look back. This mindset has served as a true source of inspiration for me personally. Additionally, Ella would have me as a guest speaker for the prayer breakfast given by her church, Bailey Temple Church of God in Christ. It initially was held on-site in the church's basement, but became obvious to me that the place was too small for a woman like Ella. I suggested that she consider moving from the basement to somewhere else more accommodating. She did, and the breakfast grew to over 2,000 persons in attendance. I, too, was challenged to move a ministry from my local church to a different, larger venue. I obeyed and the conference grew. Respectfully, Ella and I both know how to listen to people who listen to God.

Anyone who reads HERstory will be tremendously blessed and will be inspired to run and see what the end is going to be.

ELLA
"A TAPESTRY OF PROMISE"

Affection from Rev. Will Williams, Jr., Tampa, FL

On a summer day, Ella noticed me walking down the street going to visit my mother. My emotions were off the chain. Ella said to me, "I don't usually pick up grown men, but God told me to pick you up because, baby, you look so pitiful!" When she dropped me off at my mother's house, she left me by saying, "Keep coming to church and God will continue to bless you."

That following Sunday, Ella saw me and gave me a ride once again. This time, it was to church. She began to talk to me, asking me poignant questions about my life and my lifestyle; my story. Somehow, the conversation shifted and she suggested that I was in need of a new wardrobe. She handed me her telephone number, but also told me that I needed help. Her parting statement to me that day was, "Keep going to church." She encouraged me to learn more about God above anything else.

As I continued to attend church, I began to grow in God and gained knowledge in the teachings of Jesus Christ. Ella continued to encourage me. Honestly, she never stopped. She also informed me that she was praying for my success. Through our conversations and her encouraging words, she learned that I was a tailor. She once said, "I could tell you were smart because no one can make garments like what you're wearing." It was around that talk that I learned she had retired and opened a clothing boutique. As a result, I was able to serve her clientele with my skills as a tailor.

Over the years of continuous work with Ella's exclusive clientele, I have had the opportunity to grow and become more successful by having been a recipient of Ella's wisdom in the retail. As a mentor, she always maintained high standards and required these standards of me in my professional, personal, and spiritual life, as well.

Ella is one of those rare people who God has chosen to provide supportiveness and respect, and show that she is non-judgmental of others and their personal choices. Rather, Ella has a powerful way of being a blessing to all sorts of people with diverse backgrounds and uplifts the true and living spirit of God.

To God be the glory! I thank Him for her, and love her much more than she would ever know. God bless you, Mom! And thank you—Ella Gordon—for being my light.

"I am a person through other people. My humility is tied to yours."
-Zulu (Ubuntu) proverb

Chapter 8
World Tour Because of God!

"I have great respect for the past. If you don't know where you've come from, you don't know where you're going, I have respect for the past, but I'm a person of the moment. I'm here, and I do my best to be completely centered at the place I'm at, then I go forward to the next place."
—Maya Angelou, African American Poet, Memoirist,
and Civil Rights Activist

Family

Family

Acquaintances

Tyler Perry

Quincy Jones

Malcolm Jamal-Warner

Muhammad Ali

Rick James & Jo Marie Payton

Berry Gordy

Tyne Daly

Acquaintances

Ann-Marie Johnson &
Beverly Johnson

Oprah Winfrey

Marla Gibbs

Courtney B. Vance

Vivica A. Fox

Smokey Robinson

In Her Travels

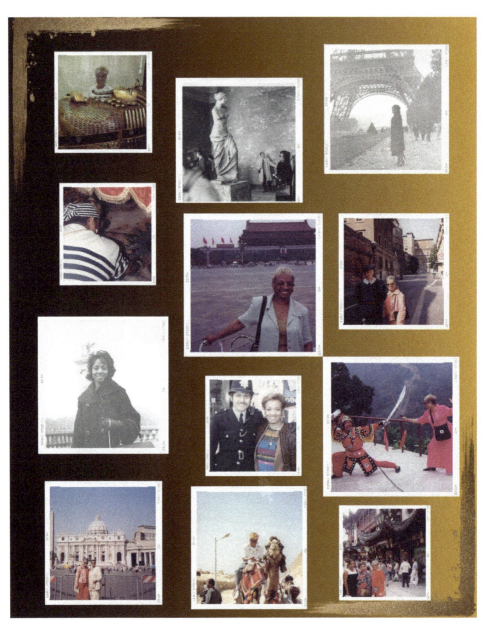

In Her Worship

...and, so it is

Afterword

THE STORY OF Ella B. Gordon is a portrait of faith, defeat, and resilience which has been converted into transformational leadership within the Church of God in Christ as an ordinary servant realizes her purpose as deemed by the Holy Spirit. From my lens, I have presented her thoughts advanced to a time accepted by our society as post-pandemic, when face-to-face interactions require us to move with sensitivity, awareness, and introspection. This conversational style of social engagement, ethical caring, humanization, and high regard for spiritual refinement best served us in telling her story.

These attributes extend far beyond one's own self and explores the relationship of Ella's spiritual influence, which yields her triumphs. Even though several leadership styles emerges relative to her servant leadership, it was Ella's transformational leadership during her life journey that I found worthy of sharing with hope of inspiring others. While social and internal defeat continued to be a challenge, Ella was able to persevere and overcome barriers that threatened to impede her progression. More remarkably, she persists in maintaining her relationship with God by relying on her abiding faith.

Acknowledgments and Contributors

I know how to live on almost nothing or with everything.
I have learned the secret of living in every situation, whether
it is with a full stomach or empty, with plenty or little. For I
can do everything through Christ, who gives me strength.
-Philippians 4:12-13 (NLT)

WHEN AN UNASSUMING meeting prospers into a relationship that forms a sisterhood between women, as they exchange wisdom and wit that accompanies accolades and adversity, it transforms into a blessed connection that couple's admiration and supportiveness.

Graciously, I extend my deep appreciation to Ella B. (Agnew) Gordon for trusting me to tell HERstory. The unique ties that brought us together exist because of Desma Reid-Coleman of who I feel an incredible sense of thankfulness for her friendship.

There is also heartfelt gratitude for the following people for making time to talk with me, offer feedback and knowledge, present ideas, lend expertise, provide both material and moral support, as well as show genuine kindness in some benevolent form as I worked through this project, *The Winding Path of a Shero's Journey*. Alphabetically listed are those extraordinary individuals:

Dr. Marcia Tate Arunga

Demetria J. Bennett

Louis Coles Benton, II

Linda C. Brown

Rick Cartier and Robbin Gordon-Cartier

Reverend Brian T. Coles

Gloria J. Coles

Dr. Thomasina L. Cook

Dr. Evelyn Ford Crayton

Evangelist Phoebe Elliot

Allie Howell Freeman

Missionary Sharon B. Griffin

Doris L. Hullum (childhood friend of Ella Gordon)

Janaté Solar Ingram

Seaborn Johnson

Ashley Perry

Betty L. Perry

Rebecca Reilly

Bishop J. Drew Sheard, Sr.

Alisha J. Taggart

Taheera B. Talbi

Bernadine C. Taylor

Reverend Arthur B. and Mrs. Jackie S. Todd

Belinda Wilson (friend of Ella Gordon)

Jo Yudess

Tanya Zabinski

Several indispensable contributors provided their gifts of time and skillfulness to facilitate a story being shared to encourage, inspire, and shed light in a world where there is darkness. My appreciation is extended to the following: Jerome Agnew, John Agnew, Kenneth and Sharon Holley, and Reverend Frank D. Thompson, III.

Sincere appreciation to Alexis P. Onyszkiewicz of Absolutely Poshee for curating the creative fabric of images to digitally capture Ella's journey.

Warmest thanks is extended to Phyllis A. Walker (educator, published creative writer and freelance editor) for her inimitable gift, encouragement, and hours adding an irreplaceable sense of realization to fulfilling my literary purpose during this chapter of my life.

> *"Let gratitude be the pillow upon which you kneel to*
> *say your nightly prayer. And let faith be the bridge*
> *you build to overcome evil and welcome good."*
> —Maya Angelou

Endnotes

1. Oveil Hamilton, "*Sanctified Revloution*", (UP Books, 2021) 22-23, 122-127, 135-136

2. Adrienne Waks, Eric Winer, *Breast Cancer Treatment a Review* (Journal of the American Medical Association 2019) 288-300

3. Adrienne Waks, Eric Winer, *Breast Cancer Treatment a Review* (Journal of the American Medical Association 2019) 288-300

4. Cheryl Holt, Annika Kyles, Therese Wiehagen, "Development of spiritually based breast cancer educational booklet for African American Women (Cancer Control: Journal of the Moffitt Cancer Center 2003), Vol. 10 No. 5 sagepub.com/DOI/pdf/10.1177/107327480301005506

5. Clyde Yancy, *Commentary on COVID-19 and African Americans*, 2020

6. A Tradition of Prayer and Celebration, kingcountypb.com/history

About the Author

"I will bless the Lord at all times: his praise
shall continually be in my mouth."
-Psalm 34:1 (KJV)

RAISED BY PARENTS Commodore Coles, Sr. and Bernice Henderson Coles, Carolyn Coles Benton was born in Flint, Michigan along with four siblings.

She received a Bachelor of Arts in Sociology at Grambling University in Grambling, Louisiana, followed by a master's degree in the field of social work from the University of New York at Buffalo. She met and married graduate classmate Louis C. Benton. Carolyn is the proud mother of two children, Taheera Talbi (Sam) and Louis II (Courtney); and one grandson, James.

Carolyn remains forever grateful for the love and support from her late husband, Louis, as well as her parents—whom unfortunately did not live to witness her doctorial commencement ceremonies, nor the culmination of her debut book release.

Her expansive career includes three decades in health care administration at Roswell Park Cancer Institute (*currently Roswell Park Comprehensive Cancer Center)* in Buffalo, New York. She also served on the faculty and staff of Bryant & Stratton College (Amherst, Buffalo, and Orchard Park campuses) in Western New York. Her national memberships include: Order of Eastern Star (Prince Hall Affiliation, New York State Jurisdiction), The Order of the Golden Circle (New York State Grand Assembly), The Links Incorporated, and Zeta Phi Beta Sorority, Inc.

In her spare time, she continues to enjoy hand quilting, playing the piano and studying the harp.

Printed in the USA
CPSIA information can be obtained
at www.ICGtesting.com
CBHW081446201223
2798CB00003B/5/J